No More Betrayals

Apuk Ayuel Mayen

Cover Art by Abul Oyay Deng Ajak.

To Tharpham,
And The Ones Lost.

You are gone too soon.

TABLE OF CONTENTS

INTRODUCTION: WHAT THE HEART KNOWS

This collection of twenty-five poems is set in South Sudan's turbulent past and present, land, and people. The poems cover an array of topics ranging from the author's life as a refugee, a record of the war in South Sudan and Sudan, nationalist sacrifices, a tribute to essential personages in the recent history of South Sudan and beyond. It also provides a commentary on the political and social systems. In a sentence, this book is an exploration of, and a soulful reflection on, the complexity of South Sudan.

This book is neither a diagnosis of what is wrong nor a prescription of how to fix a broken society, but a presentation of the beautiful mess we call life, of what the author has seen about this particular society. It is a protest of sorts, a tribute, a caution, a plea to humanity to be more human than the record has shown so far. It is about death, renewal, and continuity through a variety of ways.

It is best to read this book as a historical record. One of the poems pay homage to John Garang de Mabior, South Sudan's liberation hero who died exactly six months after he ended 20 years of war with Sudan. Another depicts, Yousif Kwa Makki, the fierce liberator from the Nuba Mountains who dedicated his life and died trying to draw the world's attention to the suffering of his people. Another poem eulogizes, Kuol Adol, the Ngok Dinka chief slaughtered by the Missiriya of the Sudan for insisting on staying on his ancestors' land. All these poems reflect the moral challenge of how far man needs to go to achieve "freedom;" what kind of freedom; what one has to destroy to rebuild; and at what price.

Some of the poems can be heartbreaking in the story they tell. The poem, "Kömiru a Paka", a rendition of the tragic tale of land grabbers run amok in the town of Juba is humorous and mournful at once. The incident in which the author's maternal ancestral land was seized to the point of eviscerating the burial grounds where her grandmother had been laid to rest not so long before, captures a familiar story, a tragic colliding of a mismanaged state and individual rights.

This collection showcases a true journey, not only the physical flight that the author undertook as a child, together with part of her family, to escape the brutality of a regime in Sudan but also a journey of the mind and heart thereafter. The heartache of the limbo in which refugees find themselves, caught between the physical refuge and spiritual presence at home is unmistakable. It so artistically paints the predicament that every refugee person will be familiar with, that of physical absence from home and the constant intellectual and spiritual commute back and forth between the birth home and the not-so-home of refuge.

These poems demonstrate how culture is not an object that refugees forget or fail to grab at the stressful moment of departure. Instead, of all the things a fleeing person cannot leave behind or forget, one's culture, memory, identity, and creativity are primary.

For readers who see language, the crafty use of words, as an art form, people who find beauty, hear music and song when they read or listen to poetry, this book will come as a bit of a surprise. It is simple and yet captivating, using the unlikely material to speak of weighty subjects and above all, coming from an unlikely literary person, a young career civil servant. The author is a diplomat by profession, but one that has carried her culture, historical sensibility, love of a country and pride in her ancestry, and has used this cultural baggage, for lack of a better term, as the backdrop to her poetry.

This book is not unique in the sense that most South Sudanese writers in different disciplines come from similar backgrounds and use that background as the material for their literary creations. But this book will be one of the only very few books that converse so eloquently with the everyday. It covers different issues, from death to the celebration of life, nation to the village, government to people, the telling of lies and the truth, betrayal and caring, songs and jokes, memory and forgetfulness.

For this reason, it will most probably be more readily accessible to people who are in tune with the cultural and historical context of South Sudan, though readers from other parts of the world will find something in this book that will intrigue, inspire, enlighten and entertain them. It is indeed one of only four books of poetry of its kind that I have been privileged to read closely and to find utterly invigorating.

Jok Madut Jok
Juba, 2018

SONGS OF LAMENT

THUS HE LEAPT

Thus he leapt:
Dust his carriage;
Pain his ammunition;
Revenge his motivation;
And death his ambition;
Leaping into obscurity.

God's wrath unleashed, he leapt;
Thirsting, starving, damned:
Quenched when innocence bleed;
Sated when carnage overfeed;
And lauded when wickedness breed;
Leaping into history.

GUILTINESS

He sold his soul for six pennies,
But how 'bout them night visitors?

The girl whose voice is dripping torment,
Whose eyes are exploding pipelines of
Life clinging fury and
Death hunting joy.

The boy whose hands are bleeding bullets,
Whose soul is projecting thunders of
Piety-destroying ferocity and
Pain-absolving sacrilege.

He sold his soul for six pennies,
But how 'bout them night visitors?

He feigns sleep
For nightmares enliven the dead.

IN THE BELLY OF RIVER NILE

In the memory of the more than 200 civilians who lost their lives in the White Nile fleeing Malakal on January 13, 2014.

We ran away
From the blazing fires of hate;
For what else motivates the killing
Of the most vulnerable of us?

We ran away
From the flying bullets of greed;
For what else inspires the murder
Of the most productive of us?

We ran:
Women, children, the elderly, and
Those carrying the yet unborn.
We ran until
We can run no more.
We ran up to the riverbanks.

We cried:
"Oh sweet River Nile
Won't you carry us to safety?
Oh sweet River Nile
Won't be our refuge in fear?"
...And the river offered us a boat.

Overcome by the will to live and
Fear of death fast approaching,

We jumped, swam and
Cramped into the boat.
Some of us lay on top of others,
We didn't mind. We were finally
On the way to safety
On the other shore.

We breathed lighter and sighed heavier.
We even mourned the loss
Of loved ones senselessly killed.
And we rested for a moment,
Only for but a moment.
Then, we were too many.

We were too many
Who entrusted our lives
To a feeble boat.

We were too many,
Too heavy
To reach the shore.

We were too many
So we found our safety
In the belly of River Nile.

No More Betrayals

Those streets lining
Remembrances of timeless sweetness, are
Now lined with our commingled corpses.

Those trees holding
Etches of timeless commitments,
Now no more than ash.

Laughter shared by the pure-hearted
Budding-buddies of lifetimes past and present,
Now muted forever by the drums of war.

Brotherhood fused in fields of play,
Nurtured in shared pasture lands,
Now torn asunder by the supremacy of creed (greed).

Marriages consecrated in exchanges of sacred cattle
Cemented through precious gifts of daughters,
Seeding nations united by blood;

Betrayed?!

Remember the laughter,
Once inspired by innocence,
Now spoiled by greed (creed).

Remember "Friends Forever,"
Once etched in hearts,
Now blinded by hate.

Remember sacred life unions,
Once perpetuated in blood,
Now shed by revenge.

No More Betrayals.
No More Betrayals.
No More Betrayals.

Ma Don't Cry

Oh, *Ma*, don't you cry;
Your lament is piercing my mind.
Though I am your last-born,
I will stand in the gap, and
Restore you.

May *Nhialic* increase my power
That I may clothe your nakedness.
May *Nhialic* increase my might
That I may feed your hunger.

May *Nhialic Wa*,
Who sees the purity of my heart,
Help me defeat those bent on ravaging, and
Pillaging your abundance.

Oh, *Mankhoc*, don't you cry;
Your wailing is piercing my heart.
Though I am your last-born,
I will stand in the void, and
Restore you.

---

* *Ma* is the word for "*mother*" in the Dinka Language.
* *Nhialic* means "*the one above*" and it is the word for the all encompassing deity in the Dinka language.
* *Wa* is the word for "*father*" in the Dinka Language.
* *Mankhoc* means "*mother of people*" in the Dinka Language.

8

MARKED BROTHER

Oh, sweet brother, you are no more,
But only yesterday you cared for my every need.
My sweet brother, they say you are now a traitor;
But no eagle can soar beyond
The heights of your patriotism.

Brother, brother,
They say your marks testify of treason
To country and creed!
But isn't there a mirage clouding their eyes?

Ironically, my brother, they say this of
Marks of manhood and courage,
Marks of beauty and dignity,
Marks of strength and integrity.

Catastrophic, my marked brother!
Your countless sacrifices and valiant contributions,
Are somehow overshadowed by your marks.

Oh, sweet brother, you are no more,
But who would care for my every need?
Brother, brother, you are now a traitor!
Who would be both armor and
Shield for our beloved country?

BELOVED

With tears in my eyes and
Sadness in my heart, I leave you, Beloved.
On the wings of The Memphis
Your day of darkening, I flee;
Plucked, as if a fruit ripe for savoring.

For the watchmen guarding
Your precious gates, prayers
To imbue them with valor, flood my heart.
For the people besieged
Within your walls, soft whisperings
Of sweeter tomorrows, echo with my every breath.

…And the watchman says:

"Why so soon my dear?
Go, I will await your return.
"They think they are devouring
Our beloved, but there is a
Divine plan to reseed her."

...And I say: "I will go, but linger
Close enough to oil your lamp,
Kindle your hope, and
Praise your valor."

[Juba, South Sudan: December 18, 2013]

Relics of Sacrifice

Hollow eyes, empty heart,
Whiplash and a heavy brow;
Father sold his soul to feed us.

Sullen eyes, heart full of emptiness,
A milk gourd and a broken back;
Mother bound her soul to free us.

Smoky eyes, broken heart,
A scarlet lace, and a barren temple;
Sister prostituted her body to educate us.

Hardened eyes, heart full of brokenness,
A badge of dishonor, and a scar of shame;
Brother pawned his body to escape us.

A sacrifice is a noble act,
But seldom sweet is
Bread baked in bitterness.

Songs of Protest

NOT JUST A WOMAN

I give you life,
I give you bread,
I give you refuge,
I give you comfort.

But I bleed, and
As I bleed,
You stand guard,
Afraid to defend me.

But I am humiliated, and
As I am humiliated
You stand dignified,
Afraid to protect me.

I am just a woman,
Just a woman.

As my heart races, and
My nerves tense -
He has a gun, and
I am a woman.

I better behave:
Speak softly, and
Why did I dare utter a word?
Choose silence, and
Why did I dare act defiant?

Am I deaf, am I mute?
Do I know about the bush life he's endured?
How can I dare answer him?
How do I dare ignore him?
I must be humbled.
I must be reminded
That I am just a woman.

I must guard my life,
Above my dignity.
I must endure, for he who earned me freedom,
Has the sole right to oppress me.

What is life, if not freedom to breathe,
To think, to speak, to live?
What is life, but blood freely flowing
Through veins dignified and intact?

You are only a woman,
Just a woman.

Be careful of the lurking danger
In the eyes of
An oppressed man,
A depressed man.

Be wary of the imminent fury
In the weakness of
A dispossessed man,
A traumatized man.

Stand and be downtrodden.
Prostrate and be spared.
Choose life or choose dignity, and pay.
Either way, you are just a woman.

I give you life,
I give you bread,
I give you refuge,
I give you comfort.

But I bleed, and
As I bleed,

You stand guard;
Do not be afraid to defend me.

But I am humiliated, and
As I am humiliated,
You stand dignified;
Do not be afraid to protect me.

I am not just a woman;
I am every woman.

I am your caring mother,
Your sweet sister,
Your precious daughter,
Your loyal wife, and
Your gentle lover.

I give you life and sustenance.
I propel you through the generations.
So bleed for me, stand guard for me;
Defend me.

My dignity is yours.
Fear not. Protect me.
I am not just a woman;
I am every woman.

THE KINGMAKER

The oracle speaks:

"O' Kingmaker,
You enthrone and dethrone
With skill and at will.
But does the throne whisper your name?

"Do make and break,
You are a mere servant of history.
Though temper your dreams of ascension
For they will be your demise.

"Do also know that your
Cunning inventions
Are precedents to be applied
On your judgment day."

"O' good people of the land,
Hail the king but be wary of the kingmaker."

And the good people ask in unison:
"But who is the Kingmaker?"

Kömiru a paka!

For Beloved Grandma Poni Tongun Bilal

Ponique, *Yang*,
May the wind clean the face of your grave, and
May lalob trees crown your head.

Yang, did you hear the rumbles of guns?!
Did you see the ashes of huts?!
Kömiru is burning in your wake.

Rest! Rest! The roots of trees will honor you.
Let your spirit roam over the land
Evaporating the blood before it stains.
Kömiru is transmuted in your wake.
Kömiru a paka![†]

Consolation is for the living
Dispossessed and desolate,
Driven out to shelter another brother, and
Their graves exhumed
For the burial of another mother.

But the cycle of life continues:
Birds sing songs they sang for the ancients, and
Children sing songs
You sang in another tongue.

Retribution is for the living
Embittered and embattled,
Restrained in wise deference
To future justice, with hopes resting

---

[1] Yang (o), is a feminine term of endearment close to beloved/dearest in the Bari language, it is either used for mother, beloved wife, and or a daughter.

[2] *Kömiru* is a name of a Northern Bari Village. It means 'Lion' in the Bari Language. *A paka* means 'is finished/destroyed' in the Bari language.

On the soft wind of change.
A sleeping lion lives to roar another day.

Rest! Rest! The roots of trees will honor you.
Yango, let your spirit roam over the land
Evaporating the blood before it stains.
Kömiru is transmuted in your wake.
Kömiru a paka!

Ponique, *Yang*:
May the wind clean the face of your grave,
Instead of my hands.
May lalob trees crown your head,
Instead of my flowers.

Thirty-two steps to the northeast, and
Thirty-five steps to the northwest.
The sun rises in *Kerek** and sets in *Lurit*.
The wind reaches you from *Lado*.

Yang, the roots of trees will honor you,
For the living will always serve
The needs of the breath life gifted them.
Kömiru a paka!

---

*Kerek/Kujur, Lurit and Lado are names of mountains in Northern Bari area of South Sudan.

GIVE THANKS

For Thanksgiving Holiday

We give thanks
For our ability to brutalize
Gains us salvation.
We give thanks
For our fortitude to dispossess
Gains us land and riches.
We give thanks
For our destiny is to inherit the earth,
Albeit destroyed and destitute.

We give thanks
For our miscalculation:
Creates disease,
Perverts seeds,
Poisons water sources,
Exterminates peoples, and
Destroys heritage.
But these are the expected collateral.

When will we give thanks for our shared humanity?
When will we extend our borders beyond our bellies?
When will we understand that no person is an island?
When will we understand that our downfall
Will be our creation?

When will we realize that the dehumanization
We think only fathomable in Congo, can, and may as
Well, be visited upon our psyches, bodies, and souls?

When will we understand that our veins of life are interconnected?
When will we know that –
Brutalization cannot bring about salvation,
Dispossession does not confer ownership, and
The human instinctual motivation to survive

21

Should not be underestimated,
For it will trump the security of luxuries.
If we have ears
We'd hear the spirits of the ancients
Disturbing the peace.
No, it is not an earthquake,
It's a spirit quake,
Warning you to heed the call to penance.
Beware lest the age of atonement expire and
You are found with your blood-stained
Everything, with even nourishment, tainted.
Do you not know that the soil and even the oil, are
But decayed remains of ancestors?

Let us give thanks
To every seed, every fruit
Every flesh, and
Every spirit that
Inspires and perspires,
Transpires and expires,
To give us life.
Let us give thanks,
Not for that which annihilates,
But for that which enlivens.

Until July 9th

A piece of bread, my child;
Let me fill my hunger,
Until July 9th.

A piece of cloth, my daughter;
Let me cover my nakedness,
Until July 9th.

Come July 9th,
The *mundukurus* will no longer
Sit on our head.

Come July 9th,
The *Khawaja* will no longer
Provide our bread.

Come July 9th,
The revolution will no longer
Be betrayed.

A bottle of *dawa*, my sister;
Let me mask my wounds,
Until July 9th.

A bottle of *Aaragi*, my daughter;
Let me drown my sorrows
Until July 9th.

Come July 9th,
In self-governance, we'll only have
Our selves to incriminate.

Mundukurus is a colloquial Juba Arabic word meaning "*Arabs.*"
Khawaja is a colloquial Juba Arabic word meaning "*white people.*"
Dawa is a colloquial Juba Arabic word meaning "*medicine..*"
Aaragi is a colloquial Juba Arabic word for a type of South Sudanese local alcoholic brew.

Come July 9th,
For self-sufficiency, we'll only have
Our resources to allocate.

Come July 9th,
The revolution turned government will only have
Our people's interest to incorporate.

HEAR MY CHANT

For Referendum

Yes, I have been downtrodden
For your ascendancy.
Yes, I have been suppressed
For your burgeoning.
For God, Creed, and Nation:

A God that sanctions my obliteration,
A creed that negates my identity, and
A nation that disavows my citizenship.

Hear my chant: the fight is over,
I will determine my destiny.

Creed needs no external validation,
But springs from the fabric of our beings.
God is not a possession of some,
But lives in the spirit within all that is life.
A nation is not an imposition,
But the choice and formation of peoples.

Hear my Ululation: the battle is won,
I will determine my lot.

Is your God a respecter of peoples?
Can this nation house multiple creeds?
Will this nation restore me, full citizenship?
Do I remain rejected or self-eject?

These questions occupy my mind
As I contemplate my choice,
Understanding the past, and
Leaving it behind.

Hear my stomps: forward marching
I will determine my future.

You are absolved,
My brothers, my sisters -
Fruits of my great aunt's womb,
O' seeds supplanted by "others;"
Completely absolved!
For my sake, and
For my enlightened self-interest.

For bitterness eats away my flesh
Before yours, and so:
It is not about you,
But about my destiny,
Lot, and future.
Not about you,
But about my dignity,
Humanity, and rights.

Hear my chant:
Yes, I have been downtrodden
For your ascendancy.
Yes, I have been suppressed
For your burgeoning.
The fight is over,
I will determine my destiny.

[Khartoum, Sudan: October 2010]

26

PRAISE BE

Praise, praise,
Praise be upon them,
The chaps of the august house
Have grown some teeth!

Sharp, sharp
Sharp as they seem!
But why is the chewing so
Uneven and incomplete?

Are they teeth grown
With a healthy regiment of calcium?
Or are they merely a mouthpiece
Borrowed for a healthy course of vengeance?

Be not impressed by the game of musical chairs,
But by measurable actions bettering your lot.
History is made, how it's made,
But remains his-story; what is yours?

Praise, praise be,
But caution and vigilance be more.

Conform to the Pulse

Conform to the pulse of the people,
Lest you become a thorn in their side.
Be guided not by the greed of those
Thieving to fill already bloated stomachs,
But by the unwillingness of the famished
To trade dignity for bread.

Songs of Patriots

HERE IS HOME

"*Ma*,** where did you bury my surra†*?"
"Here."

"*Ma*, why of all places did you choose here?
Why of all places did you call it dear?"
"Because it's here."

"*Ma*,
Did you know you tied me down, and
Crowned me a clown?
Did you know you blessed me first, and
Blessed me accursed?"
"You are here."

"*Ma*,
Here where you buried my surra,
Here is home.
Here I live and die;
Here I breathe and lie;
Here I build and break.
Here I love and hate;
Here I give and take;
Here I dance and fight.
Here I scream and shout;
Here I become and be;
Here I will and create.
Here you will bury my remains.

"My sweet *Ma*,
Blessed of all that ever been.

---

* *Ma* is the word for "*mother*" in the Dinka Language and many other South Sudanese languages.
* *Surra* is the word for "*umbilical cord*" in Juba Arabic. The tradition of burial of the placenta and the umbilical cord signifies attachment to the ancestral land.

Eternal you are, and eternal I shall be;
Reborn in perpetual birthing, here.
Here is home,
Again and again, and again.
Here is home."

THEY CALLED ME KUSH

Darkness that glistened
Under the rays of Ammun,
Decorated with a twirling chain
Of water, of life.
They called me Kush,
Most beautiful,
Most trusted, and
Most endowed.

For *Min* hid in my depths
Innumerable treasures,
Blanketed with layers upon
Layers of fertile land.
I used to walk head high,
The darkest of the dark;
Unmatched, and unsurpassed.

All vied for my attention
Or so I thought!

First, they came as suitors;
Regarding my dimensions,
Sizing up my pride, and
Noticing everything that caught my eyes.

Next, they came bearing gifts,
Enticing me to need? Need?
A word so foreign
To the abundance, I know.

Well-wishers, or so I thought!

They pulled my ear
Whispered propositions
Of barter and exchange.

Took advantage
Of my hospitality, and
Remained.
Permanent guests? Nah!

More like leeches,
Living on my blood,
Like termites,
Won't stop until
All my substance is sapped, and
My frame is broken.

The conquest had begun,
My child! It had begun.

They came one after the other –
Turks, Arabs, Anglo Saxons and
Their myriad of proxies.
And me, Kush.
Most beautiful, most trusted, and
Most endowed.
Am defiled, raped, and pimped.

Pimped, I tell you pimped...
Royalty brought down to muddy rags!

What was hidden in my depths,
Unearthed.
Veins of my life turned into
Channels of their poison.

And my children,
Your ancestors
Were displaced, and
Wrest into slavery.

Then came:
A day after night after day after a night of:

Exploitation, and dehumanization
Enslavement, and slaughter,
Wars and murders,
Genocide and ethnocide.
Ashes to ashes, dust to dust and
The rest you know.

At least the versions told to you
By those to whom my victimization, was
A burden of the spread of "civilization."
And by those to whom,
It was for the proselytism
Of a foreign god, who excuses and
Rewards the brutalization of life, life.

The brutalization of my life.
Surely, he is not my God.

I am the land drunk off
Of the blood of my children.
I am the land witness to all and
Accuser to none.
I am the land,
A testament to blessings beneath and
Horrors above;
I am the land
Here from the beginning,
There to the end.

I am Kush,
The Land of the Blacks.
Hopelessness,

Is a luxury I do not have,
For my pores are open
To water and blood.

My hope is in the wisdom of my youth.

In their recognition
That this circle of violence
Must be stopped.
In their cognition
That their unity
From Beja to Paarl, and
From Ceerigaabo to Nouadhibou,
Must be achieved.

Surely this whirlwind of destruction must cease.

Yën, Kuc/Thudan,
Yën acï mäm/gum apɛï.
Yën ŋic, nyiac a bi naŋ ëër;
Ŋogthdi a tou ke yiin, menhdi.

---

* This last stanza is in the Dinka language, and it means the following:
"I, Kush/Sudan,
I have suffered a lot.
I know tomorrow will be brighter;
My hope is with you, my child."

BLESS THE PEN OF THE PATRIOT

For Isaiah Abraham

I.
O' precious motherland
Whose veins are drenched in blood,
Close your pores, no more!

Bless the pen of the patriot;
Curse the gun of the traitor; and
Mute the voice of cowardice.

Chorus:
I see you: eyes full of tears,
Heart full of sorrows;
Grieving your finest, gone too soon.

But still, like the sun,
Your love shines equally
On the wicked and the upright.

Be just, oh sweet mother:
Deject the treacherous; and
Uproot the wayward.

II.
O' hallowed motherland,
Bless the pen of the patriot!

Why reject your prophets,
Oracles, and counselors,
The ones seeding the nation?

Why banish, prosecute, and
Send violently into martyrdom,
The ones nourishing the devoted?

37

III.
O' just motherland,
 Curse the gun of the traitor!

Why tolerate, bandits,
Defilers, and murderers,
The ones pillaging the nation?

Why not bring to justice,
To books, and
To shaming light,
The ones uprooting the earnest?

IV.
O' sagacious motherland,
Mute the voice of cowardice!

Don't you hear them sowing
Whisperings of fear in hearts weakened, and
Minds frozen by violence?
Don't you see them glorifying
Demonstrations of criminality, the undue reward
Of naming an evil, and inspiring a good?

V.
Bless the pen of the patriot,
A thousand-fold into eternity.
Curse the gun of the traitor,
 Perpetually into rust into dust.
Mute the voice of cowardice,
Even in thoughts, into oblivion.

[Pretoria, South Africa: December 12, 2012]

SOLIDARITY

Shed a tear for me,
Will you?
Give of your marrow;
Keep the abundance.

Take a stand for me,
Will you?
Battle your beast;
Rescue the fallen.

You bleed as I,
I breathe as you.
Your song my dance,
My cry your stance.

I fall,
You shatter.
I stand,
You rise.

Stand
With
Me
Dignified.

FREEDOM FIGHTER

For Yousif Kuwa Mekki

Scar-faced,
Wound laced
With courage.

Humbled by trails, and
Humanized by savagery.
Fierce in spirit, but gentle,
As only a nobleman can be.

High in stature,
Mind above matter,
Always ministrant.

Hallowed by hindsight, and
Haunted by foresight.
Taut in spirit, but shielding,
As only a nobleman can be.

A Bridge Burned

For Kuol Adol, Chief Kuol Deng Majok, Paramount Chief of the Nine Ngok Dinka Chiefdoms,
murdered by the Missiriya on May 4th, 2013.

Kuol Adol,
Of your virtues
I can't begin to speak,
For my words would prove
Inadequate.
What can I say to describe
Your unsung heroism, and
Steadfast leadership?
What do I say to pronounce
Your serenity of deep resolve, and
Certitude of unconditional love?

A life dedicated to
A beloved people.
A heart tempered
With responsibility.
No matter the clouds
You stood,
No matter the loss
You defied;
All for the Ngok,
All for the Ngok of Abyei.

The Ngok fled countless time,
But you always stayed
To be the home anchor.
A paramount chief,
A lover of land and people.
A paramount chief,
An embodiment of continuity and hope.

You persisted and lived:

To the last word,
To the last cry,
To the last drop,
To the last breath,
A life of service
Dedicated to your beloved people
The Ngok of Abyei.

Abyën du (your Abyei)
Abyën da (our Abyei)
Abyëi ë piŋ (Abyei is hearing)
Abyëi ë dääi (Abyei is watching)
Abyëi ë dhiääu (Abyei is crying)
Wët du Kuol-Adol.

Your spirit abides
In the tenacity
Of the Ngok.
Your spirit guides
Your beloved.
You accepted small
Victories
With gratitude,
But steadfast you
Remained
With eyes fixed on
Securing Abyei
For the Ngok.

Man of the people,
You gently led
Humbler than the humblest,
Most approachable, and
Most distinguished in being
Undistinguished.
From dialogue and

Engagement you never
Recanted.
You used to say that
Fate interlinked
The destiny of
The Ngok to the Missiriya, and
The livelihood of
The Missiriya to the Ngok.

The gentle fierceness
I always saw in your eyes
Shone with an eagle's determination.
You lived honorably,
But died brutally.
You will be remembered,
Added to our arsenal of ancestors
Interceding and moving
On behalf of the Ngok,
The Ngok of Abyei.

Abyën du (your Abyei)
Abyën da (our Abyei)
Abyëi ë piŋ (Abyei is hearing)
Abyëi ë dääi (Abyei is watching)
Abyëi ë dhiääu (Abyei is crying)
Wët du Kuol-Adol.

You shouldered
The burdens
Gracefully,
O' Paramount chief
Of the Nine Ngok Dinka
Chiefdoms
In the age of referendum and
The increased
Instrumentality of the Missiriya

For the forces of evil.
Destroyed neighborliness,
Shattered memories
Of bread broken, and
Grass and water
Shared.
Adding insult to injury:
Provocations!
Provocations!
Provocations!

You stood,
So we stand.
You defied,
So we defy.
We are your beloved Ngok,
The Ngok of Abyei.

O' Mercenaries of evil:
Where would you hide
When vengeance comes
Your way?
Where would you take root
When you uproot the upright?
What would be your reward?

Death is more merciful
Than the anger you've mobilized
From a benefactor.
How dishonorable,
You've cut down
The emissary of peace!
A breach of good will.
A bridge burned.
You've murdered
The one tempering

The hearts
Of his beloved people,
The Ngok of Abyei.

Abyën du (your Abyei)
Abyën da (our Abyei)
Abyëi ë piŋ (Abyei is hearing)
*Abyëi ë dää*i (Abyei is watching)
Abyëi ë dhiääu (Abyei is crying)
Wët du Kuol-Adol.

[Bole International Airport, Addis Ababa: May 5, 2013]

BLESSED SACRIFICE

I send you to the front lines;
I bless your sacrifice; and
I sing of your valor.
I will remember your stance;
I will immortalize your words; and
I will preach your courage.
Lëu be yiin kööc?˙˙

I will say,
"Leave not your homeland
To protect your life,"
But I mute my tongue
In the face of injustices, and
Hide my face in the shadows of shame.

And you say,
"I will stay, for the love of the country.
I will speak echoes of patriots
Gone long ago, resurrecting.
"Bëu ŋa a lo kööc?˙ If martyrdom knocks
My door? Who will water my seeds
If I am uprooted and ignored?"

And to the front lines, you went, blessed sacrifice.
I sing songs of your valor...
I remember your stance;
I immortalize your words; and
I preach your courage.
Lëu be yiin kööc?

---

*Lëu be yiin kööc means "Will I keep your name alive?" Kööc is a Dinka concept of
perpetuating the name of every male/female child who dies before having children (heirs).
˙ Bëu ŋa a lo kööc, means "Who will keep my name alive?"

TRIBUTE TO SPLA

For the liberation war fighters

Life for freedom,
Dreams for opportunities,
Youth for future;
Yours for mine.

A heavy load you carried,
Somehow deemed
A fair exchange
By your convictions.

You did not flinch
As duty called your name;
You gave it all
For the vision of equity.

Mighty gallant SPLA,
I salute and honor you.
I stand in awe of your valiance.

Limps for rights,
Sanity for dignity,
Afflictions for preservation;
Yours for mine.

An intractable life you led,
Somehow deemed
A worthy price
By your vehemence.

You did not hesitate
As the bush whispered your name;
You gave it all
For the pursuit of justice.

Mighty gallant SPLA,
I salute and honor you.
I stand in gratitude for your sacrifice.

Re-Member

For Dr. John Garang de Mabior's Commemoration in Washington-DC, May 2008

I.
I am the offspring of Kush,
Her pride runs in my veins.
I am the embodiment of her people's struggle,
Their plight sounds with my every heartbeat.
I am the echo of their cry for justice,
Their suffering is the driving force of my life.

I am the seed of solidarity for her dispersed children.

I am the enslaved child in Madani,
The heavy-laden bricklayer in Kosti,
The widow of war in Juba, and
The orphan whose father is war, and
Rite of passage is violence.

I am the dispossessed in Kajbar,
The displaced in Darfur,
The forgotten in Abyei,
The exploited in Port Sudan, and
The destitute in the refugee and IDP camps.

I am the wide-eyed rural boy in Khartoum,
The resilient in Akobo,
The inventive in Malakal,
The royalty of the Shiluk, and
The complexity of the Zande.

I am the wisdom of the chiefs,
The precision of the spear master,
The persistence of the sidelined politician, and
The courage of the underground writer.
I am the marginalized of Sudan.

49

II.
Now despite compromise, war, and struggle,
I am still oppressed.
In villages in the north,
I am deprived of my right to my land and heritage, and
Face imminent disinheritance and displacement.
In eastern Sudan, I am bound by illiteracy and
Every sort of marginalization, from which my only
Escape is servitude in the capitol.
The land of milk and honey, they say,
Where I live as a refugee in my own country,
Without honor or dignity.

In Darfur, I lose my humanity daily.
In the South and the border states,
My CPA is in danger of being
Yet another agreement dishonored.
For Abyei, my jewel is
A time bomb ticking conforming
To the pulse of my people's discontentment.
They say my country's economy is booming,
Yet I am the poorest of the poor.
And as long as this marginalization exists,
The struggle continues.
It continues beyond this life to the next.

And until the day when the Sudanese
Are no longer marginalized,
I am reborn.
A fire ignited in the passion sowed,
In another offspring of Kush.
That one! That one that rises from
The deepest darkness,
With a clenched fist and a loud voice:
Declaring a tribute to the spirit of the struggle

Reincarnated once more.
Proclaiming:
I am the remnant of greatness.
I am the carrier of the legacy of the struggle.
I am the living child of Sudan.

III.
I have seen a New Sudan,
A land merry with the sun
Where diverse nations and
Peoples partake of its abundant fruits.
A New Sudan free of all discrimination and
Marginalization,
Where justice and peace reigns.
And in my toil to make it a reality,
I re-member…
I re-member the legacy of my predecessors, and
Internalize it as my heritage,
A legacy, for my striving and struggle.

And in this a day of re-membrance,
I accept my duty and commit
To the deeds necessary to fulfill it.
I re-member…
I re-member…
I re-member…
I re-member Battalion 104,
Volcano Battalion and Katiba Banat.

I re-member the New Kush Division,
The Cadres in Bilfam,
The contributions of Musa Kuwa Idriss, and
The Red Army.
And I charge you brothers and sisters to re-member…

Re-Member the difficult days of the struggle.
Re-Member to feed the children and widows of our martyrs.
Re-Member the slogans of the revolution.
Re-Member, our promise to the people.
Re-Member our commitment to the vision.
Re-Member our duty and loyalty to the cause.

IV.
Re-membrance is an action, and
Not a thought.
That which was dismembered
Is now re-membered.
That which was disintegrated
Is now re-integrated,
Re-vived, re-claimed, and re-lived.
Re-Member through works, not words.

Re-Member!
Embrace this passion.
Embrace this duty, and
Become the embodiment
Of our people's Struggle.
The echo of their cry for justice and peace.
Re-Member!

Be-Come, I… Be-Come, I
I am John Garang
I am Joseph Oduho
I am Kerbino Kuanyin
I am Yousif Kuwa
I am William Deng Nhial
I am Ali Abdellatif
I am Abdelfadil Almaz
I am William Nyuon Bany
I am Arok Thon Arok

I am Ngacigak Ngaculuk
I am John Kulang
I am Martin Manyiel Ayuel
I am Francis Ngor
I am Dauod Boulad
I am Ali BGuatala
I am Emilio Tafeng
I am Ager Gum
I am Thon Ayii
I am Father Seterno Ohure
I am Gelario Modi
I am Emmanuel Abur
I am Aquilla Manyuon
I am Anyar Apiu
I am Akuot Atem
I am Gai Tut
I am the countless martyrs and
Innocent casualties of the struggle

I am the offspring of Kush, of Sudan, and
Though I am no longer breathing,
Striving for a New Sudan.
I am reborn through you and,
Through your duty and deeds,
As the struggle continues.

Acknowledgments

Tharpham (Nyale Gatkuoth) poetry drew us together once upon a time, long past. I am saddened that you will not be taking New York's A train to Barnes and Noble to purchase and read this collection. Your silent admiration was my muse for many years, and your encouragement was foundational in the development of my voice. I dedicate this book to you. Your untimely death is still a shock, but your memory lives on.

To Jok Madut Jok, and my sisters Achol and Aluel Mayen thank you for your constant cajoling to publish and for your belief that this voice must be amplified. You have been great fans since day one. To Jok Gai, thank you for taking the time to read early manuscripts, translate and transcribe some of the Dinka phrases in some of the poems. To Uncle Bek Awan, thank you for your input in Dinka transcription and translation.

To Jervase Yak, thank you for cautioning me on the traps of perfectionism in a resonating and admonishing way, a turning point. To Ambassador. Moses Akol, I am appreciative of the countless hours you've given to discussing and commenting on many of the poems in this collection. Thank you for your perspective, and any shortfalls are attributed solely to me sticking to my voice and style; "some people's kids!" To Ambassador Dr. John Yoh, thank you for the close reading, thorough analysis, and profound encouragement.

To the many friends I cannot mention here, I am grateful for your support.

Made in the USA
Monee, IL
04 March 2021